Explorers of the American West

EXPLORATION
AND DISCOVERY

The Conquest of Mexico
The Early French Explorers of North America
Exploration of the California Coast
The Exploration of the Moon
The English Colonization of America
The European Rediscovery of America
Explorers of the American West
Explorers of the South Pacific
The First Voyage Around the World
The Journey of Lewis and Clark
Pathfinders of the American Frontier
The Sea Route to Asia
The Spanish Exploration of Florida
The Spanish Exploration of South America
The Spanish Exploration of the Southwest

EXPLORATION
AND DISCOVERY

Explorers of the American West

The story of the men who explored and
surveyed the west, from John C. Frémont
to John Wesley Powell, Clarence King,
George Wheeler, and F. V. Hayden

Kelly Wittman

Mason Crest Publishers
Philadelphia

Mason Crest Publishers
370 Reed Road
Broomall PA 19008

Mason Crest Publishers' world wide web address is
www.masoncrest.com

First printing

1 3 5 7 9 8 6 4 2

Library of Congress Cataloging-in-Publication Data
on file at the Library of Congress

ISBN 1-59084-049-6

EXPLORATION AND DISCOVERY

Contents

Exploring the Colorado River

ON AUGUST 27, 1869, a hero of the Civil War stood at the site that would one day be called Separation Canyon, between what are now the states of Utah and Arizona. For three months, he and the nine men in his exploration party had faced the perils of the wild. One of their four boats had been lost in the rapids of the Colorado River, and supplies were running low. One of the men had dropped out and headed home after only a month, and now the others were becoming fearful of what the future held.

The Civil War hero was not afraid. His name was Major John Wesley Powell, and he had faced fear many times. When the Civil War had started in 1861, Powell had joined the Union army. At the battle of Shiloh, he had been struck in the arm by a cannonball. The wound was so bad that his arm could not be saved, and doctors amputated it just below the elbow.

After the war ended, Powell and his wife Emma settled in Illinois, where he taught at several colleges. He was also named curator for the museum of the state's Natural History Society. Powell liked teaching, but after traveling extensively in the Midwest, he realized that he wanted to go farther— he wanted to explore the West via the Colorado River. At age 35, he set out to prove his theory that the river had cut great canyons into the earth over thousands and thousands of years.

During the Civil War John Wesley Powell rose in rank to lieutenant colonel. However, after the war he preferred to be called major, a lower rank. He was addressed as Major Powell for the rest of his life.

Powell had heard stories about people who had died on expeditions on the Colorado, but he was determined to find a way. He spoke with anyone he could find who knew the surrounding area, especially the Native Americans, whose languages and cultures he had studied as a professor. He knew that small boats would have to be used in the descent of the river and went to Chicago to supervise the building of four boats of his own design. Powell first tested them in

John Wesley Powell

John Wesley Powell was born in 1834 in Mount Morris, New York. His father, Joseph Powell, was a Methodist preacher. Like most Methodists at that time, Joseph Powell was a vocal opponent of slavery, teaching his son that the institution was evil. For his stand against slavery, the young John Wesley Powell had been beaten up by classmates and forced to leave school. A private tutor named George Crookham was hired to teach the boy, and it was this man who sparked John's love of the natural sciences.

Joseph Powell wanted John to enter the ministry, but Powell was determined to become a scientist instead, and he worked hard to pay his way through several colleges in the Midwest. Morality was still a guiding force in his life, however, and when war between the North and the South became inevitable, Powell hastened to answer the call.

Lake Michigan, then had them loaded onto a *flatcar* and transported to Green River Station in Wyoming Territory, where his expedition would begin.

Powell's 1869 journey took him 1,037 miles from Green River, in the Wyoming Territory, to the Virgin River in the Nevada Territory. Along the way, the party passed through the Grand Canyon, fighting the dangerous rapids on the Colorado River. At some points, the walls of the canyon were a mile high.

To accompany them on their trip, Powell and his brother Walter chose not men of science, but men of nature—mountain men who knew how to live off the land. These men craved adventure and agreed to work for little or no money. Their lives were full of drinking and wild parties—activities that the religious Powell did not condone. He was willing to work with them, however, for the good of the expedition. The crew assembled at Green River City in Wyoming for several weeks of preparation. Powell trained them in the use of *topographical* instruments and flag signals. They assembled the tools and supplies they needed and launched their voyage on May 24, 1869.

Powell led the fleet in a boat named *Emma Dean*, after his beloved wife, who at times accompanied him on expeditions. She waited this one out at home, however, because Powell had decided that it was too dangerous. Emma had complete faith in her husband as an outdoorsman and was not afraid for his life, even when some newspapers reported that the entire party had been killed in the rapids of the Upper Green River. All over the country, people became fascinated with Powell's journey and waited anxiously for news of the exploration.

The men in Powell's crew had no way of knowing just how dangerous the trip would

John Wesley Powell was an expert in conchology, the study of mollusk shells. His collection of clams and mussels was the most extensive in the state of Illinois.

be. Day after day, they shot the rapids of the Colorado. When the current was too rough, they were forced to unload the boats and *portage* them over land. The work was exhausting and, at times, emotionally draining. The immense Lodore Canyon struck fear in the hearts of some

Major Powell helped create the Bureau of Ethnology, which was devoted to the study of different cultures, and was its first director. He devoted the last years of his life to studying the dwindling cultures of the Native American peoples.

of the men. In a letter written to the *Chicago Tribune*, Powell spoke of the nerves of steel required in exploration: "It has taken several years of mountain climbing to cool my nerves so that I can sit with my feet over the edge and calmly look down a precipice 2,000 feet. And yet, I cannot look on and see another do the same. I must either bid him come away or turn my head."

On August 10, 1869, after months of rowing and hiking, they finally reached the Little Colorado River, which is the entrance to the Grand Canyon. This would be the greatest test of their endurance. For days, the relentless rapids tossed about the boats and the men who clung to them. Heavy rains and flooding made this stretch of the voyage even more treacherous, but Powell and his men were still able to marvel at the sheer beauty of the Grand Canyon. At some points, the walls of the canyon were a mile high. When Powell discovered the remnants of Indian camps, he knew that other humans had inhabited the rough terrain.

Now, as he surveyed Separation Canyon on August 27, 1869, he was approached by three of his men. Bill Dunn and the brothers Oramel and Seneca Howland warned the Major, "we will surely all die if we continue on this journey." The three had decided to try to hike out of the canyon and walk across the Shivwits Plateau to the Mormon settlements. They begged Powell to join them, but they could not convince him to abandon the expedition. The next morning, the three men left the group.

Major Powell and his five remaining men then ran the last two major rapids of the voyage. On August 29, they reached the mouth of the Virgin River. Powell and his party had traveled more than 1,000 miles. The settlers who met them there were astounded to see them alive, for the entire party had been presumed and reported dead. It was not the daring Powell and his men who had perished, however—it was the three men who had left the expedition party only two days earlier. Climbing out of the canyon, Dunn and the Howland brothers had been slaughtered by Shivwits Indians, who mistook them for the killers of one of their women.

This was but one of many fatal mistakes that would be made in the exploration of the American West.

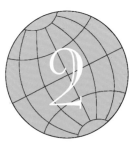

A wagon train moves west. As the United States expanded its territory during the first half of the 19th century, immigrants who wanted land were encouraged to travel west to settle in the Oregon Territory and other sparsely populated areas.

Manifest Destiny

THE JOURNEY of Major Powell and his men illustrates just how dangerous expeditions to the West could be. Why, then, were so many people—not only men, but women and children as well—willing to leave the comforts of the "civilized" East behind?

There were many practical reasons. America experienced a rise in the birth rate in the early part of the 19th century and also an increased rate of *immigration* from Europe. In the period from 1800 to 1850, the population of the United States grew from five million people to more than 23 million. Since most people at that time made a living through agriculture, finding new land was always a priority. Much of the land in the unsettled West was inexpensive, or even free.

Many people who *emigrated* from such countries as Germany and Ireland did not feel safe and comfortable in the eastern United States. Those of the Catholic and Jewish faiths were routinely discriminated against. In the West, immigrants were able to set up their own communities and keep their religions and traditions alive.

In 1839, the United States suffered an economic *depression*. In the cities of the East, many people were unable to find jobs. Poor people were often exploited in dangerous workplaces, such as coal mines and *sweatshops*. They saw the passage West as a way to gain land and freedom. They could work for themselves rather than for someone else. Some families that had never farmed before came to ruin, while others found success and prosperity.

The opportunities for *commerce* in the West seemed endless. Businessmen knew that farming communities would need general stores, feed stores, and sawmills. Industrialists saw the chance to mine new land. And *maritime* merchants wanted to open ports on the West coast in order to trade with such Pacific countries as China and Japan.

Making the expansion of the 1840s possible was new technology. Railroads and steamboats made travel faster, more comfortable, and more convenient than ever before. And the telegraph, invented in 1844, made long-distance communication possible for the first time.

By 1850, nearly 4 million people had moved to western territories. Before these people could make the trek, however, someone had to pave the way.

> **When James K. Polk took office as president in 1844, there were 4,000 Americans living in Oregon Territory and only about 800 Americans living in California. These people were eager to become part of the United States.**

Explorers were needed to open passages to the West and to create maps and books that would help others in their journeys. Government, the newspapers, and the culture combined to create an idea that was irresistible to many young men—the idea of Manifest Destiny.

A journalist named John L. O'Sullivan coined the phrase "Manifest Destiny" in 1845. He meant that the push west by settlers was happening so quickly and had so much momentum that it was now inevitable that the United States would stretch all the way to the west coast. In time, some white people began to feel that God meant for them to have all the land they wanted, even if they had to steal it from Native Americans. Some considered the Indians to be savages who had to be converted to the Christian religion. Others didn't care whether the Native Americans lived or died, so long as they kept moving west, out of the way of white settlers.

Of course, not all white people who went west hated Native Americans or wanted to steal from them. Many explorers befriended the Indians, and some, like John Wesley Powell, pleaded with the U.S. government to be fair and humane when dealing with them.

The idea of Manifest Destiny was widely accepted. People thought that by extending the borders of the United States, they were extending the boundaries of freedom and liberty—at least, for those of European heritage.

To Southern slave owners and the politicians who rep-

Under President James K. Polk, the United States continued its policy of Manifest Destiny. He declared war on Mexico, which resulted in the addition of more than 500,000 square miles of territory, including the present-day states of California, New Mexico, Arizona, Utah, and Nevada. Polk also negotiated the disputed boundary of the Oregon Territory with Great Britain, setting the border between the United States and Canada at the 49th Parallel.

resented them, Manifest Destiny was a way they could expand slavery without being bothered by *abolitionists*. Yet in the end, many African-American families were able to find their first taste of freedom in the West by managing their own farms or working on ranches.

> **Before the Mexican War, Mexico had found colonization of its northern territories to be almost impossible. Mexican citizens did not want to move there out of fear of warfare with Native American tribes like the Apaches.**

Manifest Destiny was also the reasoning behind the United States' war with Mexico. In the early 1840s, much of the American southwest was still controlled by Mexico. Many in the U.S. government felt that Great Britain, which claimed the Pacific Northwest as its own, would *ally* with Mexico and make future U.S. expansion impossible. James K. Polk was elected president in 1844 in part because of his promises to help the country grow. Two years later, the Mexican War began. By the time it ended in 1848, the United States had added more than 500,000 square miles of territory in the West, including the present-day states of California, Arizona, New Mexico, and Nevada.

The way was open for expansion to the Pacific Ocean. Americans just needed someone to show them the path.

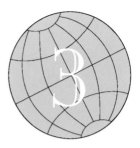

The Pathfinder and the Mountain Men

JOHN CHARLES Frémont was one of the most interesting and colorful explorers of the mid-19th century. Frémont's scientific achievements were matched only by the daring adventures he undertook in the pursuit of knowledge.

Frémont had been born in 1813 to a woman whose own parents were wealthy *socialites* in Virginia. Frémont's father, a poor French immigrant, refused to marry his mother. In those days, that was a heavy burden to bear for a child. Although his mother's family provided a comfortable home for him in Charleston, South Carolina, John was embarrassed by the circumstances of his birth and resolved to overcome them by performing great deeds. From his earliest childhood, John C. Frémont's ambition was apparent to all who knew him.

Frémont attended college in Charleston and quickly made important social connections. A *diplomat* named Joel Poinsett was impressed with the young Frémont and helped him get his first assignment—surveying the southern Appalachian Mountains. Poinsett had helped to set up the Topographical Corps of the United States Army, the purpose of which was surveying and mapmaking. Frémont was commissioned a second lieutenant in the Corps and was named assistant to the French scientist Joseph Nicollet. In their exploration of the upper Missouri and Mississippi rivers, Nicollet proved to be an excellent teacher. Frémont learned not only how to make maps, but the survival skills necessary to lead successful expeditions.

The poinsettia plant, often used as a Christmas decoration, was named in honor of John C. Frémont's patron, Joel Poinsett, who was the first U.S. ambassador to Mexico. Poinsett first saw the plant during his first diplomatic visit to Mexico.

Missouri senator Thomas Hart Benton was impressed by the work of Nicollet and Frémont. Benton was one of the foremost expansionists in the country, exerting a strong influence on the Manifest Destiny movement. He and

Missouri Senator Thomas Hart Benton was one of the leading supporters of Manifest Destiny. He liked John C. Frémont and hoped to use the charismatic young officer to further the cause of U.S. expansion.

Frémont became friends as well as political allies. Benton was soon dismayed to learn, however, that his 16-year-old daughter, Jessie, had fallen in love with the charismatic Frémont. He quickly arranged for Frémont to be sent on a supplemental survey of the Des Moines River, but absence made the young hearts grow fonder. As soon as Frémont returned in 1841, he married Jessie Benton against her parents' wishes. The senator was angry at first, but realized there was nothing he could do. Soon, his affection for his son-in-law returned.

In the meantime, the health of Joseph Nicollet had been failing, and Frémont pushed hard to be allowed to take over his *mentor's* duties. His ambition paid off when President John Tyler, at the suggestion of Senator Benton, appointed him to lead an expedition to the Rocky Mountains.

Frémont arrived in St. Louis on May 22, 1842, along with a German named Charles Preuss. Even though Preuss hated the outdoors, he had decided to become a *cartographer*, or mapmaker. He served Frémont well on many explorations. Frémont also met the famous mountain man Kit Carson at this time and asked him to join the expedition.

Frémont and his crew set out across the prairies for the mountains. They traveled along the Oregon Trail, and then along the south fork of the Platte River. They explored the mountain wall from St. Vrain's Fort, Colorado, to Fort Laramie, Wyoming. At Fort Laramie, Frémont and his men prepared to cross over the Rockies. They took the south pass along the Sweetwater, Frémont commenting that the mountains there were no more intimidating than Capitol

Jesse Benton Fremont was the daughter of Senator Thomas Benton. She was 17 years old when she ran away to marry 28-year-old John C. Frémont. For the rest of her life, Jesse would aid and support her famous husband. She helped write the reports to Congress that gained Frémont the nickname "the Pathfinder."

The Oregon Trail

The Oregon Trail was a 2,000-mile route west followed by thousands of pioneers in the 1840s and 1850s. Starting from towns on the Missouri River like Independence, Westport, and St. Joseph, wagon trains would follow the trail westward to where the Blue River meets the Platte River. The Oregon Trail then followed the south bank of the Platte to the Sweetwater River, which led to South Pass in Wyoming. Continuing along the Bear, Boise, and Snake rivers, travelers eventually reached the Columbia River. This took them to land in the Oregon Territory, which included the present-day states of Washington and Oregon.

Hill in Washington, D.C. Reaching the Wind River Mountains, Frémont climbed what he thought was the highest peak and planted a homemade flag adorned with an American eagle. It was a symbol of all his father-in-law believed in, and Senator Benton rejoiced in hearing accounts of the trip.

Frémont's report on the expedition was rushed into print to accommodate the next session of Congress. The Senate had 1,000 extra copies printed for eager readers. Newspapers all across the country published dramatic accounts of the adventure. Although the mission had accomplished little, scientifically speaking, it had a great impact on the American people. Thousands were inspired to contemplate their own journeys west.

At around the same time, a navy commander named Charles Wilkes was undertaking a survey of the western coastline of North America. Senator Benton next asked his son-in-law to connect "with the surveys of Commander Wilkes on the coast of the Pacific Ocean, so as to give a connected survey of the interior of our continent." In other words, the senator wanted Frémont to find a way to link the ports of California to cities in the midwest, thus paving the way for trade. The Oregon Trail would be mapped and laid out for the people who would surely follow. The expansionists in Congress were also counting on Frémont to scout out locations for a string of forts that they wanted to build.

In the spring of 1843, Frémont again left from St. Louis. His crew consisted of 39 mountain men and hunters, including Charles Preuss and Kit Carson. Frémont soon discovered, however, that the first mass migration to Oregon and California had begun. He met many parties on the Oregon Trail, including priests heading for a mission in Bitterroot Valley and William Gilpin, who would go on to become the governor of Oregon. Frémont was encouraged to see others following his lead, but he wanted to break new ground. He led his crew south along the Kansas River instead of the Platte River and crossed the Laramie Plain to the Great Salt Lake. The party then followed the Snake River to the Columbia River and Oregon. Leaving his men in Dalles, he went on alone down the Columbia to Fort Vancouver and met up with Commander Wilkes.

His government mission over, Frémont decided to do some exploring of his own. On November 25, 1843, he

Kit Carson

Christopher "Kit" Carson was one of the most famous western mountain men. He was born in Kentucky in 1809, and grew up on a farm on the Missouri frontier. He ran away from home when he was 16 years old to join a trading expedition. By the time he was 23, Carson was a trapper, hunting throughout the West.

After serving as Frémont's guide, Kit Carson worked as a scout during the Mexican War (1846–1848). From 1853 to 1861, he worked as an Indian Agent in Taos, New Mexico. He fought with the Union army during the Civil War, rising to the rank of general and leading troops against hostile Native Americans in the southwest. Kit Carson died in 1868.

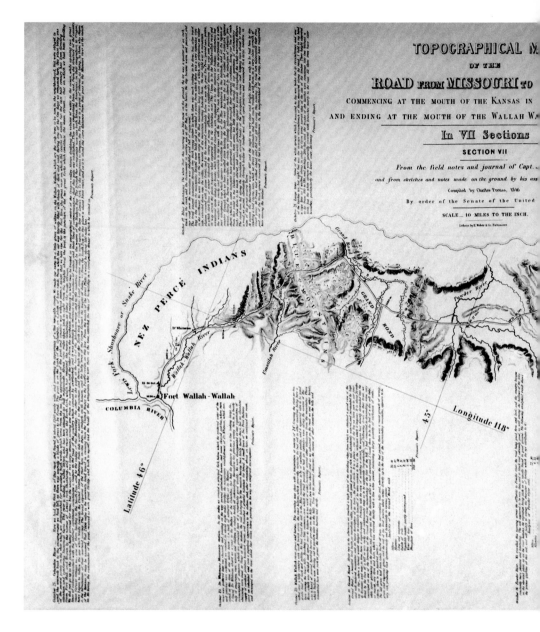

rejoined his party and headed south, looking to prove the existence of the Buenaventura. This was a legendary river that was said to lead to the sea. If the river did exist, Frémont wanted to document it. If it didn't, that was some-

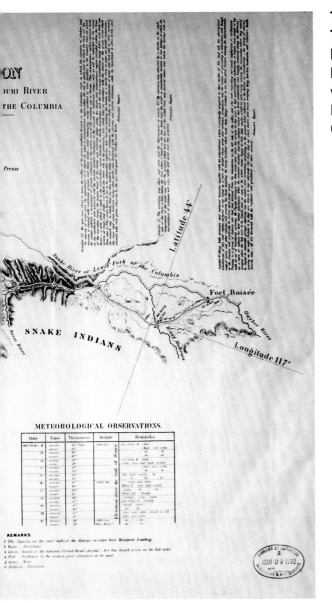

This map of the Oregon Trail was drawn by Charles Preuss, a member of Frémont's expedition. It was used to illustrate Frémont's report to Congress in 1846.

thing that the president and Congress needed to know.

For 30 days, the Frémont party fought their way across the Sierra Mountains. Winter had begun, and the men needed every ounce of strength they could muster to complete the trek. They were hungry and cold. One man went insane; another deserted the group and ran into the forest. Many in the group felt that they would never emerge from the mountains alive. Finally, however, they climbed down and returned to civilization as heroes. No evidence of the Buenaventura had been found.

Unlike Frémont's first journey, his expedition of 1843–44 provided a wealth of scientific information. The specimens and data he collected created a vivid image of the West. His partner, Charles Preuss, drew his first map of the West to present to Congress, and his wife Jessie, a talented writer, helped him to polish his report. It went through six printings and was widely read. The report fired

John C. Frémont continued to have an interesting life after ending his days as an explorer of the West. In 1856, he became the first presidential candidate for a new political party, the Republican Party. Even though Frémont did not actively campaign for the presidency, he still received 33 percent of the popular vote, losing to James Buchanan, a Democrat from Pennsylvania. Four years later a Republican candidate—Abraham Lincoln— would win the presidency.

the imaginations of potential emigrants in America and even in Europe. Frémont soon became popularly known as "the Pathfinder."

Frémont's life continued to be an adventure. During the Mexican War, he was court-martialed, found guilty of insubordination and conduct prejudicial to good order, and dismissed from the army. He went on to become a millionaire during the California gold rush, ran for president in 1856, and served as a Union general during the Civil War. However, by the 1870s Frémont had lost his money, and he died a forgotten man in 1890. Still, the bravery of the Pathfinder and the mountain men who assisted his expeditions had paved the way for explorers to come.

Clarence King's 1867 expedition covered a 100-mile-wide area that followed the 40th Parallel. This was the route along which the transcontinental railroad was being built. The group passed through parts of six states, and saw many wonders, including Pyramid Lake in Nevada.

The 40th Parallel Survey

IN THE 1840s and 1850s, much had been accomplished in the field of exploration. Expedition parties had gone farther west than many had thought possible, and mass migration to the West had begun. Still, many of the accomplishments of these decades were symbolic rather than practical. The mountain men may have been intriguing characters, but most of them did not have the intellectual skills necessary to convey their knowledge to the American public. It was time for the men of science to step in.

Yale College in New Haven, Connecticut, was arguably the most prestigious college in the country by 1860. Its Sheffield Scientific School had been founded in 1852 to

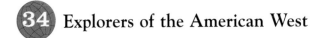

facilitate the graduate work of its most brilliant scientific minds. Its goal was American progress—and that included westward expansion.

A young man named Clarence King entered the Sheffield Scientific School in the fall of 1860. He was good-looking, athletic, and most of all, confident. Those who knew him felt that he was destined for greatness. King was excited about the new kind of education that the Sheffield Scientific School offered. He did not want to spend his days hidden away in the Yale libraries. He wanted to learn directly about science through action and adventure.

In 1862, King and a classmate, James Gardner, set out to join the California Geographical Surveys. There, King impressed the influential *geologist* William H. Brewer. It was while working with Brewer that King learned much about the exploration trade. Word of King's energy and creativity eventually trickled back East. The brash King had no doubt that he would some-day lead a survey for the U.S. government, even scribbling in one notebook: "The U.S. Interior Survey C. S. King, Supt." Those who knew him

Clarence King's mother, Florence, was a skilled linguist who taught her son to be fluent in several languages. This was helpful to King in his later expeditions, because he came into contact with people from all over the world.

Clarence King

Clarence King was born in 1842 in Newport, Rhode Island. Though his wealthy father died shortly after his birth, King had been brought up in upper-class Newport society. It was while studying at Yale that he began his career as a scientific explorer.

After completing his western surveys, in 1878, King published *Systematic Geology*, a book that is considered a classic in geography. In 1879, he became the first director of a new government department, the United States Geographical Survey.

King's public life was unconventional, and so was his personal life. He married an African-American woman 20 years younger than he was. This was unheard of in the mid-19th century. They had five children together.

King was ill for many years before his death on December 24, 1901. The handsome aristocrat from Newport is now recognized as one of the greatest scientists of the 19th century.

never doubted that he would make this dream a reality.

When King arrived back at Yale, he secured the support of Colonel R. S. Williamson for his plan for a survey of the 40th Parallel. In 1866, armed with letters from Williamson and many of his academic mentors, he went to Washington, D.C. to convince Congress to finance the expedition. In 1867, Secretary of War William Stanton appointed him to

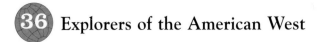

A member of Clarence King's geological survey of the 40th Parallel works while seated on a rock at Shoshone Canyon and Falls in the Idaho Territory. This photograph was taken in 1868 by Timothy O'Sullivan, a member of the expedition.

lead the 40th Parallel Survey. He was expected to report regularly to the Chief of Army Engineers. King was only 25 years old.

To accompany him as his crew, King chose men who had been trained at Yale and Harvard, some of whom had also attended the most advanced German universities. John Gardner, who had become one of the most respected field topographers in the country, turned down a job at Yale to join him. All of the geologists and **botanists** King chose for the expedition were part of a new breed of scientist—progressive-minded people who were not bound by traditions. He also brought along a talented photographer, Timothy O'Sullivan.

The goal of the survey was to examine and describe the geological structure, geographical condition, and natural resources of the land extending from the 120th **meridian** eastward to the 105th meridian, along the 40th parallel of latitude. The expedition would sweep through Nevada, Utah, Colorado, and southern Wyoming. King intended to map this area with a new accuracy, study the possibilities for economic development along the lines of the Central and Union Pacific railroads, and advise the military on subduing the Native American population.

The party of 11 sailed from New York on May 1, 1867, crossed the Isthmus of Panama, and arrived in San Francisco on June 3. The crew then went to Sacramento to train for the rigors ahead. On July 3, they started east over the Sierras and established their first camp at Glendale, about 30 miles from the new town of Carson City, Nevada.

Over the next few months, King and his group worked to create an accurate map of an area of some 15,000 square miles. While the geologists and topographer did their work, Timothy O'Sullivan photographed the Pyramid Lake area.

Unfortunately, **malaria** infected the survey party, and

The King of Diamonds

In 1872, some five years after his survey of the 40th Parallel, King proved himself a hero in one of the biggest financial scandals of the 19th century. Two prospectors, Philip Arnold and John Slack, came into San Francisco with diamonds that they claimed to have collected from a remote mine. A group of San Francisco businessmen formed a company to develop the deposit, hoping to sell stock to the speculation-mad public.

King heard about the "discovery" and decided to investigate. He visited the mine, which was located near the borders of the present-day states of Utah, Wyoming, and Colorado. King immediately realized that it was a fraud. All of the stones lay on the surface—they had simply been planted there by the prospectors.

King traveled as quickly as he could to San Francisco and demanded that the stock sales be stopped, thereby saving thousands of people from financial ruin. He was praised as a hero, and nick-named the "King of Diamonds."

King fell ill. Even those in the party who weren't sick suffered terribly from the intense heat. One man was so hot, he tried to shelter himself in the shadow of a telegraph pole. King knew he had to move fast to save the expedition. He moved his men south to the Stillwater Ranges. There, King was struck by a bolt of lightning. He survived, but his right arm and side turned brown. King refused to give up. Slowly, his health and the health of his men returned, and they continued with their survey.

As winter approached, King went to Virginia City, Nevada, where he made his report to the army. Aside from making great progress in mapmaking, the crew had collected 2,000 rock specimens and examined dozens of mines.

King never revealed his marriage to a black woman to his family. The ceremony was performed under the name of "James Todd." His wife did not know his real name until shortly before his death.

They had also established 300 barometrical stations that allowed them to determine the pressure of the atmosphere and forecast the weather. Despite malaria and the cruelties of nature, the survey had been a great success. Over the next few years, King and his crew continued to document the West, serving both the army and their country.

The Last of the Great Explorers

GEORGE MONTAGUE Wheeler was born in 1842, the same year that John C. Frémont began exploring the Rocky Mountains. By the time Wheeler graduated from West Point in 1866, John Wesley Powell was exploring much of the last wild areas of the West, and soldiers like Wheeler— a second lieutenant—were flooding the job market. Wheeler was an arrogant young man, however, who had no doubts about his own abilities. He was determined to produce a topographic map of the entire region west of the 100th meridian.

Many of his peers found him to be pompous and rigid, but no one could deny Wheeler's success at West Point, where he graduated sixth in his class. He was a hard worker who strove to impress his superiors. He married into wealth and set about making his dreams of Western exploration a reality.

Wheeler was assigned to General E. O. C. Ord's command in California. There, he studied the science of military mapmaking. In 1869, he led his first expedition through eastern and southern Nevada. The journey covered 82,000 square miles and took five months to complete. This land had been traveled by many explorers before Wheeler, but he was the first to document it using topographical instruments.

John Wesley Powell's civilian operation had been an incredible success, but Wheeler knew that the military had to respond to needs not met by the private sector. Large-scale, accurate mapping was absolutely vital to the future of

John Wesley Powell was a competitive man who was always outspoken in his criticism of his rivals. Even he, however, admitted that George Wheeler's work "ranked with the best that has ever been done."

the U.S. military in the area. Wheeler's hardiness and bravery made him the perfect man to lead an expedition into dangerous Apache and Paiute territory. His ambition allowed him to shrug off rumors of Indian hostility. Wheeler's confidence also came from the knowledge that he had the full backing of the military. Many officers were not happy that the rival Interior Department had paid for other surveys of the West. The army hoped that Wheeler would strengthen its position in the West.

At the age of 30, on May 3, 1871, Wheeler took charge of an official expedition to make geographical surveys west of the 100th meridian. He was assigned to explore and map the area south of the Central Pacific Railroad, in eastern Nevada and Arizona. He was also ordered to study the cultures of the Native American peoples who inhabited the land, as well as the mineral resources and climate. To assist him in these tasks, Wheeler recruited a team of 30 men, made up almost exclusively of civilian scientists.

Aware of how important good publicity had been for earlier surveys, he asked Clarence King's photographer, Timothy O'Sullivan, and a reporter, Frederick W. Loring, to accompany the expedition. Loring proved to be not only a good reporter, but quite an amusing traveling companion. He made the men laugh with his impersonations of Crowitch, a Shoshone Indian chief, and of Brigham Young, the leader of the Church of Latter-day Saints. The men were thankful for his humor.

The party would need all the comic relief it could get. While exploring Death Valley that summer, temperatures

Wheeler was no friend to the Native Americans. He called the Indians "barbarians" and "savage assassins" and was reported to have strung up an Indian boy by his thumbs. Wheeler did not believe that the United States should pursue peace with the Native Americans. He advocated a much harsher policy in which native land was simply taken away and the Indian cultures left to die out. When his opinions were reported by California newspapers, it somewhat diminished his reputation.

rose to 120 degrees. It was called Death Valley for good reason: several men had perished there while looking for gold and silver. In his diary, Wheeler wrote, "The stifling heat, great radiation, and constant glare from the sand were almost overpowering, and two of the men succumbed near nightfall." The men were eventually revived, but one had been unconscious for over an hour.

After overcoming the hardships of Death Valley, the expedition team began its exploration of the Colorado River. The Army wanted to extend troops as far into the region as it could. Wheeler and his men set out in three riverboats. They traveled upstream, as a fast downstream ride would not have allowed for the detailed documentation Wheeler planned. It was hard work to paddle and push the boats against the current of the Colorado, but the beauty of

The western surveys were filled with dangers. This is a photograph of Fred W. Loring, the reporter who accompanied the Wheeler expedition, with his mule. According to Timothy O'Sullivan, who took the photo, the picture was "taken about 48 hours before he was brutally murdered by Apache-Mohaves. [Loring] was returning to the East with a mind stored with rare adventures and scenic wonders."

the canyons amazed the exhausted men. Their boats often *capsized* in the roaring rapids, and toward the end of the journey, there was very little food left. Finally, the expedition party reached the mouth of Diamond Creek. Their long trek was over.

Perhaps the greatest accomplishment of the Wheeler survey was the photographs taken by Timothy O'Sullivan. Very little is known about this man, except that he took the first photos of this rugged and treacherous land. They were reproduced in newspapers across the nation and are still used in history books to this day.

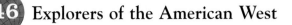

In the years to come, Wheeler became embittered when his scientific methods were called into question by other explorers, such as John Wesley Powell. Many felt that it was time for the Army to get out of the surveying business and let the civilian scientists take over. Wheeler continued with his work, however, setting up astronomical observatories and experimenting with contour maps. He produced 71 maps and published hundreds of reports on everything from geology to history.

One of Wheeler's greatest rivals was the explorer Ferdinand V. Hayden. Born in 1829, Hayden had grown up on a farm, where he became something of a self-taught naturalist. At the age of 16, he began teaching school. At Oberlin College, his classmates thought him a bit of a dreamer. Although he worked hard, he was impractical. No one expected him to go very far in life.

Though the college that Frederick Hayden attended, Oberlin, was a hotbed of antislavery activity, Hayden never seemed to have any interest in any cause outside of his own education.

The one man who did have faith in Hayden was his mentor, James Hall, the author of *The Paleontology of New York.* (Paleontology is the science of studying fossil remains.) Hall allowed Hayden to assist him in his work and live with him while he studied for

A noon meal in Ferdinand V. Hayden's camp at Red Buttes, in the Wyoming Territory, August 24, 1870. Hayden is seated at the far end of the table; he is wearing a dark jacket and facing the camera. This photograph was taken by W. H. Jackson, who was the official cameraman of the Hayden survey and would become famous as a photographer and painter of the American West.

his medical degree. When Hayden graduated in 1853, Hall sent him on his first expedition, to the Dakota badlands. Hayden enjoyed working with Hall, but soon broke with him to conduct his own expeditions.

In 1854, Hayden secured financial support from a wealthy family and returned to the Dakotas for a two-year

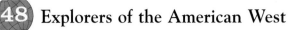

study. His exploration covered most of South Dakota and Montana. Whereas the scientists who had gone before him had been concerned with general aspects of geology, Hayden concentrated on a specific area, the Cretaceous strata. (A strata is a layer of earth formed by the deposition of sedimentary rocks.) He and his partner, paleontologist Fielding Meek, made a good team, and they achieved almost overnight success in their field. They created the first stratigraphic model for the American West, setting the standard for future scientists.

Hayden broke with European tradition by using simpler language to explain his discoveries. This made his work more easily accessible to the average American, but brought criticism from others in his field, especially John Wesley Powell, who wrongly believed Hayden to be uneducated and crude. In fact, Hayden was the most precise of scientists, and his vast collection of vertebrate and invertebrate fossils was a giant leap forward for the natural sciences.

The largest annual grant F. V. Hayden ever received from the federal government was $25,000. Hayden was only granted the money after a struggle with General Land Office Commissioner Joseph B. Wilson, who had wanted the funds for his own survey.

Hayden served as a surgeon in the Civil War, then

The area that Hayden and his party explored in 1871 is now Yellowstone National Park. The park sprawls over the states of Wyoming, Idaho, and Montana.

returned to the Dakota Badlands to collect more fossils. Unlike George Wheeler, Hayden got along well with the Native Americans. He respected their cultures, and they, in turn, called him "the man that picks up stones running." He was also unlike Wheeler in the sense that he did not have the financial backing of the U.S. government. For the most part, his freelance expeditions were privately supported. When he became aware that

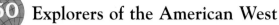

The Washburn Expedition

In August 1870, nine men left Helena, a town in the Montana Territory. They intended to travel to the Yellowstone River, in Wyoming, and prove or disprove stories about fantastic geysers, a petrified rainbow, and other tales about the area. The unconventional expedition included a banker, two merchants, and a tax collector. The Montana surveyor general, Henry D. Washburn, was their leader.

The Washburn party crossed 7,000-foot-high mountain ridges that were heavy with snow, then traveled through thick forests. The found the petrified rainbow—an encrustation of multicolored minerals—at Mammoth Hot Springs. Continuing to follow the river, the party found the Grand Canyon of the Yellowstone, as well as the geyser that would become famous as "Old Faithful."

When the Washburn party returned, its story prompted Congress to fund an official U.S. survey of the area. The leader of this expedition would be Ferdinand V. Hayden.

In 1872, President Ulysses S. Grant signed legislation making Yellowstone the first national park.

the state of Nebraska had some available federal funds, he lobbied hard for the money, was successful in obtaining it, and conducted a survey of the geological resources of the new state.

In 1871, Hayden led an expedition of Yellowstone, documenting the natural beauty of its geysers for the American public. His efforts helped convince Congress and President Ulysses S. Grant that the area was a national treasure, and, on March 1, 1872, Yellowstone became a national park. Hayden's survey of Yellowstone became the best known of the post–Civil War surveys, making average Americans aware of the science of paleontology for the first time.

Hayden continued to work for the government for the rest of his life. He missed the freedom of leading independent expeditions, but in his heart he knew that the day of the great discovery was over. White men had now walked on every area of the West, and settlers were flooding the western states.

Wheeler, Powell, and Hayden, the last of the great explorers, had served their country so well that explorers were no longer needed.

The geyser known as **Old Faithful** was photographed for the first time in 1871, during Hayden's expedition. By 1910, thanks to the work of the explorers of the American West, most of the good western land had been settled.

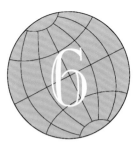

Beyond Discovery

BY THE 1870s, the age of American discovery was over. Every part of the country had been explored and mapped. Americans had familiarized themselves with the West and were now comfortable with the idea of their nation stretching from coast to coast. Mexico and Great Britain had long since ceased to be threats. Many in the U.S. government felt that it was time to concentrate on settling these areas with Americans of European descent.

Throughout this decade, the last of the great explorers continued to argue over whose surveys had been more accurate and more beneficial to the American people. John Wesley Powell and F. V. Hayden, in particular, were vicious

53

rivals, each one constantly attacking the other in reports and letters. The bickering was finally ended in 1878, when Congress created the United States Geographical Survey to coordinate all the independent surveys it funded. Clarence King was made director of this new government agency.

The explorers had opened the West and brought about many changes to the American landscape, but what did those changes mean for the West?

In 1870, buffalo hunters began moving onto the plains. There was good money to be made from selling buffalo skins and meat back East. Unfortunately, there was no control put on the number of buffalo that could be slaughtered, and within a decade, the buffalo was an endangered species. Had the U.S. government not moved in at the last minute to protect the herd, this animal would not exist today.

The West was as wild politically as it was in every other way. One day, the Utah territorial legislature was granting women the right to vote; the next, a California court was upholding the segregation of white and black children in public schools. African Americans were not the only minority that had to fight for civil rights in the West. Chinese immigrants were often exploited by industry and faced discrimination in housing and employment. The Union Pacific Railroad hired Chinese laborers for $32.50 a month—nearly $20 less than white workers were paid.

Although federal authorities estimated that hunters were killing 3 million buffalo every year, in 1873 President Grant vetoed a bill that would protect the buffalo from extermination. Soon the animals would be nearly wiped out on the plains. This photograph shows some 40,000 buffalo hides at Rath and Wright's Hide Yard, Dodge City, Kansas.

Whites across the West began to feel that the Chinese were taking jobs away from them. This led to violence and unrest.

For Native Americans, the opening up of the West was nothing short of a disaster. Throughout the 1870s, their numbers continued to decline as their land shrank and white settlers introduced diseases, such as smallpox and malaria, to the West. In 1871, Congress passed the Indian Appropriations Act, which ended the practice of treating Native American tribes as sovereign nations. All Indians were now to be treated as individuals and *wards* of the federal government. This meant that tribal structure meant

The work of explorers like Frémont, and of geological surveyors like Powell, King, Wheeler, and Hayden, opened the American West to settlement.

nothing under the law and that tribal elders no longer had the right to negotiate treaties. They might be consulted by U.S. representatives as a courtesy, but they no longer had any real power.

It was also becoming more difficult for outlaws to use the West as a hiding place. The long arm of the federal government now reached across the entire continent, and the explorers had a lot to do with that, too.

Progress was changing the face of the West on a daily basis. The railroads continued to grow at an ever-faster pace. Cable cars were introduced in San Francisco. Barbed wire was invented by Joseph Glidden and played an essential role in agriculture and ranching. New strains of drought-resistant wheat turned a once-barren desert into the breadbasket of America. In 1877, Congress passed the Desert Land Act, permitting settlers to buy public land at only 25 cents per acre.

Easterners had been warned many times about the danger and heartbreak that they might face in the West. Yet throughout the 1870s, they kept coming. Life in the West was often difficult and cruel, but for many Americans, the chance to find true individual liberty and economic freedom was worth any risk. They were thankful to the great explorers who had had the courage to show the way.

Chronology

1813   John C. Frémont is born in Virginia.

1829   Ferdinand V. Hayden is born.

1834   John Wesley Powell is born in Mount Morris, New York.

1842   John C. Frémont leads his first Western expedition along the Oregon Trail as far west as the South Pass in Wyoming; Clarence King and George Wheeler are born.

1843   Frémont and his men cross the Sierra Mountains and explore present-day Utah and Nevada.

1845   Newspaper editor John L. O'Sullivan coins the phrase "Manifest Destiny."

1854   Ferdinand V. Hayden begins a two-year exploration of South Dakota and Montana.

1856   Frémont runs for President and loses to James Buchanan.

1862   Clarence King and classmate James Gardner set out to join the California Geographical Survey.

1867   Clarence King is appointed to lead the 40th Parallel Survey.

1869   John Wesley Powell and his crew set out to explore the Colorado River.

1870   The Washburn party sets out in August from Helena, Montana, and travels along the Yellowstone River, finding many scenic wonders along the way.

Chronology

1871 George Montague Wheeler takes charge of the United
States Geographical Surveys West of the 100th Meridian;
Hayden leads an expedition of Yellowstone.

1872 Clarence King saves thousands from financial ruin when
he exposes two California prospectors as frauds; Congress
and President Grant declare Yellowstone a national park.

1877 Congress passes the Desert Land Act, permitting settlers to
buy public land at only 25 cents per acre.

1878 Congress creates the United States Geographical Survey, a
new government agency that will coordinate all surveys of
the West. Clarence King is named director.

Glossary

abolitionist—a person who is against slavery and wants to do away with it.

ally—to unite with or form a connection between.

botanist—a person who studies the biology of plant life.

capsize—to overturn on the surface of the water.

cartography—the science of making maps.

commerce—the exchange or buying and selling of goods or services on a large scale.

depression—a period of economic hard times, characterized by high unemployment and low productivity.

diplomat—a person who represents his or her country in dealings with other nations.

emigrate—to leave one's place of residence or country to live elsewhere.

flatcar—a railroad freight car without permanent raised sides, ends, or covering.

geologist—a person who studies the earth, in particular its rocks, soil, and minerals, as well as its history and origins.

immigration—the act of people entering into a new country to settle permanently.

Glossary

malaria—a disease transmitted by mosquitoes and characterized by chills and fever.

maritime—of, relating to, or bordering on the sea.

mentor—a trusted friend or guide.

meridian—an imaginary line between the North and South poles that crosses the equator at right angles.

portage—to carry a boat overland from one body of water to another or around an obstacle.

socialite—a socially prominent person.

sweatshop—a shop or factory in which workers are employed for long hours at low wages and under unhealthy conditions.

topographical—having to do with natural and man-made features of a region and showing position and elevation.

wards—people who are under the guard or protection of the government.

Further Reading

Goetzmann, William H. *Exploration and Empire: The Explorer and the Scientist in the Winning of the American West.* Austin: Texas State Historical Association in cooperation with the Center for Studies in Texas History at the University of Texas at Austin, 1993.

Lavender, David. *The Great West.* New York: American Heritage, 1965.

Marcovitz, Hal. *John C. Frémont.* Philadelphia: Chelsea House, 2002.

Milner, Clyde A. *The Oxford History of the American West.* New York: Oxford University Press, 1994.

Morgan, Ted. *A Shovel Full of Stars: The Making of the American West, 1800 to the Present.* New York: Simon and Schuster, 1995.

Internet Resources

The exploration of the West

http://www.kcmuseum.com/explor09.html

http://www.schantz.com/fremont.htm

http://www.canyon-country.com/lakepowell/jwpowell.htm

http://www.desertusa.com/magnov97/nov_pap/du_jwpowell.html

http://www.pbs.org/kera/usmexicanwar/dialogues/prelude/
manifest/manifestdestiny.html

Index

Photo Credits

About the Author

Kelly Wittmann has written a novel, as well as dozens of articles on history, art, and literature. She lives in Milwaukee, Wisconsin.